The Sounds *of the* Last Days

REVISED EDITION
HOW TO LEAD BY DIVINE SOUNDS
THE FOUR GREAT SIGNS

Alexander O. Emoghene

Table of Contents

Dedication

I dedicate this book to my dear Heavenly Father who through the Holy Spirit worked in me so strongly to deliver His precious words to His precious Church.

To my wife, Judith, and all she has done in encouragement, prayers, and her gentle way of saying, 'Go for it,' even when I took too long in prayer and preparation.

Over the year, the work of God has been appreciating in knowledge and scope. I dedicate the work to all the precious brethren who have join the ministry and have become vital encouragers, readers, students and partners in ministry among such individuals are Pastor Cosmea Kambel, Pastor Tamara Bronne, Pastor Meryl Fransman, Sister Paola Broerse Corbo and the growing CCI Family where I am the lead Pastor.

Thank you.

Acknowledgement

I would like to appreciate Dr. Don Brawley. Our meeting for lunch in Atlanta, Georgia, USA truly gave me what was needed to continue in the assignment of the Lord. You are a true friend.

My thanks also go to Denice Rafenberg leadership in Claypot Church who after a Sunday service stopped me and said, "Pastor, what about the book? Go, I will sponsor it." Heaven will keep smiling on you.

Mr. I.C. Leslie in India, thanks for your initial work of proofreading and editing. May His Grace increase in your life and ministry.

Introduction

What a time we are living in!

There has never been a time in the history of mankind that has been so fast and furious as the one we are living in. It is getting daunting as the time approaches the last days.

The Spirit of the Lord is speaking expressly to the church in every realm through many voices and sounds around the world and getting His church ready for the journey ahead. I am privileged to narrate to you what the Spirit of the Lord has impressed on my heart.

The four great signs of the last days which are thunders, lightning earthquakes, and voice, did not make any sense to me at first because I judged rather prematurely as to the relevance of this revelation to me or the church at large.

We mostly interpret situations and/or happenings as to how relevant they are to us because society has trained us to be selfish and self-centred. But in these last days, God wants to show us what is relevant to Him!

The Four Great Signs are the messages of God. His mind is revealed within the sounds created in the heavenly places. These are the causes for devastations and the ripple effects that we have on the earthly places, both seen and unseen.

Chapter One

HOW IT BEGAN

I travelled between Holland and the United Kingdom often as we carried out research on Church planting. During one of those trips, I began to sense the Lord reminding me of a book I had read. The title is "Summoned to Lead" by Leonard Sweet. I suppose it had left deep impression on me.

Little did I know, a year later, some concept I gleaned from it, will become the trigger the Lord uses to lead me into such great truth in His word.

However, prior to the above experience, I had a dream, which shook my core. It was as though I was pulled out, at the brink almost drowning. Indelibly, it led me into sessions of prolong intercession. During which, the Lord recalled these words in me "...I have commissioned you to be a writer of My messages to the church". It was a reminder of my commission to write. It was from the 18th of February 2004 when these words were delivered to me and Oh... How I have been unfaithful thus far!

As the waves gently rocked the ferry, which I had boarded from The Hoek van Holland Harbour in the Netherlands to Harwich international in the UK, I couldn't help but to be perturbed by the exuberance of a group of young people, as they celebrate the birthday of one among them. They were, to say the least, very rowdy and conspicuous in their party costume.

Amid all the noise, I began to sense the presence of God; thank God for His presence! As He continued to draw closer, I knew He intended to tell me something. Immediately I pulled out my laptop, stuck my earpiece on for some worship music, and I was amazed at what the Spirit began to pour into my heart.

He reminded me of His great Love for people and how He has been pouring out more words to the Church, for the Church to pick up and run with but how we have allowed the noise from the world to deafen our ears to His voice.

I said, "Lord, Your voice?" my rhetoric was followed by the Lord saying to me, "FAITH COMETH - The faith in my house needs to rise to new levels in order to grasp the new sound which will be entering the world from both realms."

I realised I didn't hear 'faith came,' but 'faith comes.' There is the faith that every man has been given which is '...*the measure of faith*'.

There is also the faith which comes to us by listening or hearing as it were of God's word. Faith conveyed by God's words.

We need our spiritual ears and heart to be trained, to increase our capacity to receive, retain, and understand messages from God. In this book, I am not aiming to reveal something new but to highlight the necessity to go beyond the usual with God. It is my desire to sensitize our mind and heart to the fact that God still speaks, and when humanity fails to access such information or revelation, nature will play its role in the process.

In my first edition, which was released in 2012, I gave a broad summary of these events, but now 8 years later, we see such escalation of natural devastations around the world. Such that spots on the globe, where we never thought to be susceptible to natural disasters, for example, earthquakes have become a hot stop and a reason for concern. It is was such truths and confirmation that led me to consider an updated version.

Roman 10:17 *So then faith cometh by hearing, and hearing by the word of God.* (KJV)

Roman 12:3 *For I say, through the grace that was given me, to every man that is among you, not*

to think of himself more highly than he ought to think; but to think soberly, according as God hath dealt to each man a measure of faith. (KJV)

Matthew 24: 1...*And Jesus went out, and departed from the temple: and his disciples came to him for to shew him the buildings of the temple.*

² And Jesus said unto them, See ye not all these things? verily I say unto you, There shall not be left here one stone upon another, that shall not be thrown down.

³ And as he sat upon the mount of Olives, the disciples came unto him privately, saying, Tell us, when shall these things be? and what shall be the sign of thy coming, and of the end of the world?

⁴ And Jesus answered and said unto them, Take heed that no man deceive you.

⁵ For many shall come in my name, saying, I am Christ; and shall deceive many.

⁶ And ye shall hear of wars and rumours of wars: see that ye be not troubled: for all these things must come to pass, but the end is not yet.

⁷ For nation shall rise against nation, and kingdom against kingdom: and there shall be famines, and pestilences, and earthquakes, in divers places.

Chapter Two

FAITH COMETH

It is no longer such a mystery to understand that we have mastered the art of speaking positive things and receiving blessings and great manifestation of grace by meditation, spiritual sightings, and vision in the body of Christ.

Spiritual attention from heaven is being raised concerning this coming generation. It is said to be under the onslaught of the enemy. This generation is being drowned by these last days' voices of demonic distractions, interceptions, misinterpretation, and misrepresentations. The enemy is strategic, and he's orchestrating grave distraction from the doctrines of God to hearing[1] and discerning in the areas concerning the current move of God.

---

[1] Isaiah 30:21 / John 16:13

He has poured so much noise, and sound on the mind and the eyes of the society at large, and the believers are being sucked in, no longer understanding the basic function of active listening.

Our children are filled with so much false visions. They continue to be sucked in by corrupt images from the media, social media, gaming, and the internet in general. Where all these are the invention of men, satan is using them to corrupt and hamper spiritual ear from receiving clarity from Heaven.

There's an epidemic of spiritual deafness prevailing in the body of Christ. Largely since our hearts are programmed and sensitized for visualization but the Lord in this last day will train His new leading voices in the field of "audiolization." I know! The word is new right? Audiolization is the power to understand or grasp new and upcoming trends by deep intuition. Also, it's the power to lead radical change in changing times and seasons by inner conviction.

These are high risk individuals whom God can speak to, and they will respond in absolute trust by the inner voice of instruction. Such are the leaders God is seeking now, will you be one of them?

There is a symbiotic relationship God intends for His church. It is the power of the visionary and audionary leadership. This new generation is becoming more and more frustrated and running from one meeting to another to hear a word from God with open eyes but deaf ears. God is calling for the church to retrain its hearing. It has been by and large dormant in the body of Christ. As Leonard sweet elucidated in his book "Summoned to Lead," Sight is great but can be thrown into the mirage experiences. Where after a while, one can no longer see true purposes of life. Gradually, everything becomes blurry and indistinct. Hearing, on the other hand, can hardly be mistaking or misconstrued. It continues to bring clarity in the course of time.

(prophecy)
"But they cannot hear a word from Me" says the Lord, "because their ears are not opened and most of them are not interested in opening their ears as long as some- one can make them see something else."

God wants sanctified ears to interact with; individuals who have applied His blood on their ear[2] and have truly separated their ear from iniquity, pretentiousness, assumptions, and presumptions.

Who says God still speaks even when he gets involved in the unholy works where this is a grand deception? Such individuals will sooner or later be exposed to the lies of the enemies which will prove fatal.

We seem to forget that every revelation and vision from God can build our faith. Every such word releases a

---

[2] Leviticus 8:23

7

peculiar sound, originating from the heart of God. In other words, all the revelations we will ever need to build our relentless faith, for exploits, shall come through hearing, and this we do by linking up to God who is the Source of all true revelation.

> 'to see it,' is to 'first hear it.'

So, God says 'to see it,' is to first "hear it.' 'This new generation,' He said, 'is being taken away by sight.' The enemy is propagating living by sight for such a long time even in the church, that it is now proven difficult for the Spirit to speak a word of relevance in and to the church.

Remember the story of Adam and Eve, where a word of instruction was received, and down the line, they chose to be led by sight rather than the sound words they received from God, and they both pay the price of sin and death.

(prophecy)
The Spirit of God is speaking loud and clear today to the Body of Christ. Saying, He would not replace His doctrine for such a people. If He does, He will become unjust.

The victory of the saints comes from the ability to speak the word of the Lord against contrary situations. And it results to peace, order, and control[3]. For example, in the area of divine healing, one can function

---

[3] Mark 11:23

under God's delegated authority to command sickness and disease make way for healing. One sure reason for a reduction of such power, is the inability to access God's spoken word by hearing.

THE POWER OF
THE TRANSFORMED MIND

Transformation is instigated by minds given to a process of hearing, believing, and implementing the mind of God on the earth.

The Bible claims every good and perfect gift finding expression in the earthly realms is credited to God as the source. This must be understood in a wider sense of the word, *'every,'* *'good'* and *'perfect.'* This order of endowment should establish His church as the centre for inventions and innovations.

> Transforming the mind is not going to be God's commitment, but the churches.

God desires His people, therefore, to engage Him in active listening, which in turn, will eradicate such weaknesses and lower level achievements, experienced in many Christian circles. Transforming the mind is not going to be God's commitment, but the churches[4].

This transformation is essential. The blessings channels remain open for God's good desires and plans to

---

[4] Romans 12:1-3

reach the world. Such that, God's will and the culture of heaven will eventually be a lifestyle of humanity through transformed minds.

Conformation by and large has been the hindrance of God's people. As a result, stagnation and the lack of progress are the experiences of many believers. Minds that will not break into new places and challenge themselves in new areas of listening and becoming audionaries will repel the manifest presence of God's glory.

Active listening *'transforms mind.'* It sets the tone for progress[5] before the *conformed mind* can understand it. If the Christian mind is God power to deliver men from conforming to the desires of the flesh and the depraved lifestyle of darkness to the glorious life in Christ, it means that all gifts that are currently blessings and benefiting humanity today, must come via the transformed mind (referring to the born-again child of God[6]).

When we refer to lack of hearing, it must be emphasised that God cannot be hindered nor stopped from speaking. He will still speak his desire through the church for the world. However, the church may not benefit from such transactions and interaction as it were, due to lack of transformed minds.

---

[5] Isaiah 30:21
[6] John 3:5

It is like throwing a rock into a ponder. The ripple effects of God's word having been delivered in the Church, as a unique sound, travels fast, and the effects are felt on every level in life. Sadly, the church may not enjoy the rewards allocated.

David had a new voice and technology to solve Israel's real and present day's danger packaged as Goliath. As a young man, he had experienced God in ways that had transformed his mind. "Your servant has killed both the lion and the bear; this uncircumcised Philistine will be like one of them because he has defied the armies of the living God." This was his testament. Hence David understands that process of restitution when he asked the men standing near him, "What will be done for the man who kills this Philistine and removes this disgrace from Israel?[7] Who is this uncircumcised Philistine that he should defy the armies of the living God?" When he demanded, the effects and the rewards allocated should remain in Israel.

There have been moments in history when the church has missed out on cashing in or receiving real estates and wealth transfer to build strong epi centre to house the glory of God.

However, due to lack of hearing, such revelation may remain a short while in the Christian environment,

---

[7] 1 Samuel 17:26

and it escapes or licks into the world, where the blessing is most needed in the first place.

The tragedy is the world cannot receive God sounds without a reaction[8]; in this case, a negative reaction. Remember, after Jesus prayed God to glorify His (God) name, God responded from heaven by saying, "I have both glorified it and will glorify it again"[9] The scripture attested to the fact that the bystanders thought it was thundering or an angel had spoken to him. The world system cannot interpret the voice of God. It will be two systems that will eventually clash, even in the best attempt not to do so.

Hence the church needs to commit hear from God. To not only be translators but to become interpreters. There is a great difference from when Jonah was in the boat to Tarshish to when Jesus was in the boat with the disciples. Same storm, just that one experienced destruction in the process while the other calmed the storm, and in the process, the Apostle received a profound revelation of who God is.

Transformation was the difference. Jonah knew old Nineveh, but he did not understand God's new process for bringing change. The storm and the loss trained him. Had his mind been transformed, there would have been minimal damage and loss. God is calling His church to start hearing again.

---

[8] John 16:3
[9] John 12:20-29

These last days, due to the revelation and manifestation of these 'Four Great Signs' sweeping through the earth, we shall see the whole communities, learning and receiving new ideas, concepts, creativity, and innovations. It will increase to such monumental proportion.

Again, we must emphasise that the church must master the act of hearing the voice of God not only as in the past centuries but in proceeding to higher dimension to effectively lead these changes at ease, with minimal damages.

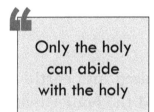

Only the holy can abide with the holy

These sounds were created as such a loud pitch and powerful spiritual technology in spiritual sound waves, moving at such force and loaded with higher revelations. There are valuable for the restructuring of the whole systems and societies when captured and harnessed by transformed minds; oh, by the way, this cannot be counterfeited.

There are no sounds in earthly places that can be louder than these sounds made in heaven. Yet, the church, made in heaven, is lagging in creativity and innovation. Why? The challenge of transformed minds.

These sounds will only submit to pure and unadulterated minds. Only the holy can abide with the holy. The ripple effects of these holy sounds and their activities will be felt by the whole world sooner or later, and the world cannot stand their powers.

We hear of disaster everywhere, even in countries where geographically are not susceptible to natural disasters, also demographic shows a higher concentration of Christian. Why is this?

Only when the holy and the transformed people of God can receive and interpret the requirements and demands of these sounds.[10]

Both the church and the world, as it was, are being trained through these four great signs discussed in this book.

These gifts made in heaven are released into earthly places through this technology called the Four Great Signs. These benefits and blessings are poured out as a result of the anointing of God on the believers in Jesus Christ.

Can you remember what happened when Laban got hooked up with Jacob? The blessing flowed in his household and on his business, and the Bible says he (Laban)[11] knew the source was from the God of Jacob.

Genesis 30:27 *And Laban said unto him, I pray thee, if I have found favour in thine eyes, tarry:*

---

[10] Romans 8:19
[11] Genesis 30:27

for I have learned by experience that the LORD hath blessed me for thy sake (KJV)

This is outstanding because Laban served idol gods, but he could not attribute these good and perfect gifts to his gods.

Genesis 31:30... *"And now you have surely gone because you greatly long for your father's house, but why did you steal my gods?"* (NKJV)

The same thing happened to the home and business of Potiphar who was the captain of the guard in ancient Egypt. When Joseph came into his household as a slave, Joseph's status did not prevent the flow of God's blessings. What happened is also outstanding because the Bible says that Potiphar's household also began to experience the favour of God. Although it is not recorded that Joseph went to the fields, but Potiphar's land also became blessed.

Genesis 39:5...*So it was, from the time that he had made him overseer of his house and all that he had, that the LORD blessed the Egyptian's house for Joseph's sake; and the blessing of the LORD was on all that he had in the house and in the field* (KJV)

For God's servant, Abraham, to see his seed and his seed's seed, he had to hear a word from God. He had to drain out the voice of nagging Sarah, the sight of parading Hagar, and the noise of crying Ishmael, in order to bring laughter into his house.

Noah had to hear the word of the Lord to be able to stand before the cruelties of 120 years and a mocking generation to build an ark without fainting. This historic drive-through is scenic, but they are waiting to happen to you right now, even better than it was then because these sounds are getting bigger and better.

The children of Israel failed in the wilderness because they shut their own ears to the Word of God. They said, *"Moses, you hear from God, and whatever He tells you, we will listen."* Secondary information will not accomplish primary results and is no good when it comes to these last times. The Spirit says, **'He that hath ear, let him hear.'Rev.3:6** (KJV)

Deuteronomy 5:25-27...'Now therefore, why should we die? For this great fire will consume us; if we hear the voice of the LORD our God anymore, then we shall die. 26 'For who is there of all flesh who has heard the voice of the living God speaking from the midst of the fire, as we have, and lived? 27 'You go near and hear all that the LORD our God may say, and tell us all that the LORD our God says to you, and we will hear and do it.' (KJV)

Chapter Three

WHEN FAITH ARRIVES

Faith moves with a tremendous force. The gates of hell cannot stop it. It is the bedrock of our confession. Faith

> **Faith is sent to make us look good and pleasant.**

is so stable that you can safely build on it. Faith is a substance. Faith has an origin; originating from the word of God, and it is sent to accomplish something perfect, having the capacity to instruct generations to come. Faith is sent to strengthen and to help us receive the blessings of God. Faith is sent to ensure we live our best life now and to please God. Faith is sent to bring us joy amid a perverse world. Faith is the door to the God-life. Faith is the word that cannot be uttered but can perform whatever can be uttered by it.

In **2 Corinthians 12:4** Paul said that he was caught up into paradise, *'and heard unspeakable things spoken which man is not allowed to utter'* (DBY)

Paul spoke of words which cannot be uttered. I agree to the fact that these are faith-filled words, full of power to change an entire generation. In these last days, worshippers need to survive on those words that cannot be uttered. Why? There is a sound from heaven that can only be captured by those who have ears to hear, and when they capture these words, they will be the ones who will manifest the glory of God in dynamic ways. They will best be prepared in leading and leadership at this time, where God is getting His church ready and for the lift off (the calling up of the church to heaven).

There is an evil rain about to fall from the clouds of evil and corrupted words. They are carriers of the dangerous elements of deception and destruction, ready to rain on the world, and there are no detergents in the human realm that can wash them off the skin and minds fall on.

However, those words that cannot be uttered will act as deep cleanser for the believer. So, entering the realms of hearing is the way to be immune from satan's doctrines at the same time, the hearer will be God's divine catalyst for greater impact on the world.

Prophetic word: - The clouds are forming already. I see people running into shelters made by man's doctrine, but this rain will miraculously corrode the roof of human made shelters to destroy those that have not received the word from the Lord. But I see the Lord within mid-air, with intercepting showers, miraculously forming and shooting out the word through flashing of thunders and lightnings with word able to cleanse the hearers, to heal and restore the hearers and these words would show us a clear direction to safety. The Spirit says he who has ear, let him hear what the Spirit is saying:

Revelation 3:22...*He that hath an ear, let him hear what the Spirit saith unto the churches* (KJV)

Chapter Four

FIVE SENSES

All the five senses given to us by God, enables us to enjoy life whilst here on earth. These senses are built for five major or primary functions which are sight, hearing, tasting, smelling, and feeling by which, we connect with our natural world.

Adding to these primary functions are also secondary functions. For example, the eye is built primarily for sight. But within the sight, the facets of shapes, sizes, beauty, colour, and many more can be perceived. Same goes for the tongue and the function of tasting. Yes! There are many

> Leadership is great when it is visionary, but God is going to raise 'Audionaries.'

kinds of taste! What about touching as a primary sense? Yes! We can sample thousands of textures around the world! The same could be said about smelling also. One can smell and differentiate billions of odours.

However, the ear is one peculiar organ where its secondary function exceeds the rest because it is the only organ that is connected directly to the brain. Hence, the effect of sound on the brain can be colossal, and the influence can either be positive or negative depending on what it is subjected to. As sound is captured, the mind of man needs to be cultured, conformed, and controlled, seeing that the brain functions as CPU (central procession unit) and the information centre of the human being.

Thus, the statement, *'you are what you eat,'* assumes lesser light compared to what *you hear,* and the rate of change that takes place when hearing becomes active is beyond what anyone can imagine.

Everybody makes a different sound. In many ways, we have been influenced by the sounds somebody else dares to initiates. The power to influence changes in one's life is directly proportionate to what is heard.

So, we are most likely to respond to the loudest and the clearest sound, and usually, we get led by them. God has chosen in these last days to released great sound from heaven. These are highly influential sounds above[12] our universe, and this sound will be heard everywhere. Often time as humans, we miss the waves of

---

[12] John 3:13

revelation sent by God, and it seems as though, nature becomes the only medium Gods has at His deposal to channel these messages. Jesus pointed out that God can raise up stone to praise His name, proving the fact that God may provoke nature when there are needs to be met in the earth.

Luke 19:38...*Saying, Blessed be the King that cometh in the name of the Lord: peace in heaven, and glory in the highest.*

39 And some of the Pharisees from among the multitude said unto him, Master, rebuke thy disciples.

40 And he answered and said unto them, I tell you that, if these should hold their peace, the stones would immediately cry out (KJV)

In another verse,

Jeremiah 10:13...*When he uttereth his voice, there is a multitude of waters in the heavens, and he causeth the vapours to ascend from the ends of the earth; he maketh lightnings with rain, and bringeth forth the wind out of his treasures.* (KJV)

Jeremiah speaks of the utterance of the voices of God and how nature responds to Him. When the Apostles in the book of Acts finished their prayers in Jerusalem during the persecution of the church, the Bible refers to a shaking that occurred because of the answered prayer.[13] There is no record of death, but the Bible says that they were filled with boldness. These were the worshipers who lived with their ears wide open to receive answers from heaven.

Acts 4:31 *And when they had prayed, the place was shaken where they were assembled together; and they were all filled with the Holy Ghost, and they spake the word of God with boldness.* (KJV)

These are the signs of our days. We must understand that the coming of the Great King is near, and every great king has a protocol: every one of his subjects must line up into place at the sound of his entrance. The mouth of the earthquake, the flashing of thunders, and the whirlwinds of tornadoes are responding to the call of God to worship. Where is man in this whole picture? We are still hard towards hearing and caught up in self-centeredness, greed, and insolence.

As believers, what are the sounds that influence us the most? The tragedy is making a sound that you cannot dance to!

What is the sound of your church? What is the sound of your assignment? What is the sound of your business? Compare that to where you want to be? Is it between a war cry and a celebration of songs for God?

---

[13] Acts.4:31

The church must see what God is saying to her. Leadership is great when it is visionary, but God is going to raise 'audionaries' in these last days to add to bring increasing value to His body to stop the devil and his cohorts the opportunity of blurring visions as we go along.

Too many people are living immoral lives that have marred them with optical illusion and false imagery. It is no wonder why some of us are thirsty because we are drinking from mirages instead of wells of living water. It has always been God's heart desire is for His children to remain refreshed and empowered with vision and revelation springing from wellsprings from the sounds of heaven.

Please note that the ear as an organ does not stop growing; an indicator to us that in hearing the Lord, we need to keep on growing continuously in influence and dominion by connecting to heavens' resources.

Company mergers are strategic to increase productivity and sustainability. They now realise that the more they harmonize, the more they are able to capture a greater chunk of the market. In essence, the better sound they will create. At one point, the most used word in corporate settings has been "*synergy*." The underlining factor to this philosophy is that companies that are making similar sounds are getting together to create a larger and more powerful sound of influence.

The believer's life is no different when it comes to hearing from God. Yes, we cannot afford to be separate from God's voice. Deciding our personal affairs, business, and marriages matters when God wants to lead and release His favour. Our personal successes depend largely on the kind of sound wave we connect with from heavens. Is your message clear, and can your listeners make out what you are saying? As a leader, the tune you play to glorify God and to lead your generation depends strictly on how much you've listened to Him. In the next chapter, we will understand the new generation leader.

Chapter Five

AUDIONARIES

These are individuals who have adapted their **leadership** style through a set of unique hearing acumen which allows them to lead the next generation into the future through a present sound culture

I made up this word 'audionaries,' with which I will explain what the Spirit of the Lord is speaking to us as a body.

Leadership in our days is going to be even more by the art of *"hearing."* It is called *"Musical-Leadership,"* where *"sound"* from heaven is allowed to creates the environment for growth and influence. It is also where active listening is utilized as a tool to maximize common interest at the same time benefitting everyone by co-ordinating our financial matters, educational growth, and national wealth. I am not talking about hiring a boys' band and staging a show at your company's "End of the Year" party. In the real sense, it is manifesting the mind and the wisdom of God in churches and in the business world by believers who are motivated and led by the sounds of God. Hearing from heaven and spending valuable time in listening before every move, will be the mark of the new generation leaders.

You cannot merge two companies that produce entirely different sounds. Oh! There will be great chaos and confusion! Christian leaders often lean toward leading God's church with visual aids, but God is calling leaders to a silent place for maximum downloads for the future.

There is going be an outburst of supernatural concepts and ideas which will change the course of the entire region because of direct downloads from the Holy Spirit. An audionary is an individual who learns and leads best at hearing. It must be admitted that good to great leadership is a combined effort of great leadership and amazing followership. Leaders cannot attain their desired height without a vital connection to the team they lead.

The hearer-leader does not get confused when the Spirit speaks because he is accustomed to dancing to the tune of heaven as it were. To be effective as leaders in the church today, it is imperative for us to hear for the next level and to see the next level. When we see the next level, then we can go to the next level.

Our actions and reactions are based on what we hear in the spirit. What we hear is translated into faith. Christians' growth can all of a sudden be hindered; they start shrinking and suffering due to spiritual attacks; they seem to be losing the fight.

This can happen to any of God's children when we fail to open our ears to Him continually. As the Scripture says,

1 Corinthians 10:12...*So that let him that thinks that he stands take heed lest he fall.* (DBY)

In essence, this call to hear is an opportunity from God to have audience with Him. It is to create huge access channels for major exploits in the earth.

'Audionaries' would speak loudly and make effective sound into the earthly realms. Powers will be given to these last-day leaders, to catapult them into the next phase of God's agenda for the church, world, and the Jews. In the book of revelation, there is a prophecy concerning two powerful personalities who wielded great powers, even nature was subject to them. Some say these will be certain human personalities that will rise up among the Jewish nation. Where this conveys irrefutable truths, I am of the view, it will be an insight into the symbiotic relationship between the kingly and priestly ministries represented in the body of Christ, in full power before He comes. They will possess unstoppable and formidable front against outside influences and will be successful against prevailing cultures of evil because they are going to audionaries. They take their source from these great four signs that have been released into earthly places.[14]

Our hunger is a reflection of what we hear. What we hear determines our drive and achievements. Do not wonder why there are so many lukewarm believers in your church who cannot command signs and wonders. We can do only what we hear. Better off, we can speak only what we hear. Note what the book of Mark says:[15]

Jesus emphasized the word "*saith*" three times, giving rise to the power of words. In this the last chapter, we shall talk on the strength of sounds words.

Hearing precedes speaking. In pediatric, speech impediment in children, often time, are a result of an impede hearing. Children who struggle with lateness to speaking would be recommended for hearing check-up. Likewise, in the spirit, speaking with power means one has to hear from God something powerful and full of faith.

It is such power and faith; the believer needs to cause the impact necessary to bring the kingdom of God in the world. The spiritual realm is not different from the natural when it comes to the primary and secondary sensory functions of the human organs.

---

[14] Revelation 11:4-6
[15] Mark 11:23

To hear in the spirit, we would have to see *"Sound"* as the primary means for the spiritual ear, but at the same time, the spiritual ear is capable of hearing many other sounds as it chooses to hear. That is why we need to be strong on the written Word of God.

Why? Our rising or falling depends on what we hear on a daily basis. Jesus declared that man shall not live by bread alone but by every word which proceeds out of the mouth of God. We must preach the infallibility of the word of God again with power[16]. We are not left in the dark why the words of Jesus conveyed such power and authority. He is the original audionary[17]

> Our hunger is a reflection of what we hear.

It was noted about Jesus...: **Luke 4:36 *They were all amazed, and spake among themselves, saying, 'What a word is this! For with authority and power, He commanded the unclean spirits to go out, and they came out.' (KJV)***

> Leadership is going to be even more by the art of 'hearing'

Why? He spoke faith-filled words, words for the full-grown adults and not for the babies. Babies cannot comprehend fully, and so they cannot speak words that will draw the attention of others. Apostle Paul says... *When I*

---

[16] John 12:49

[17] John 5:30

was a child, I spoke as a child[18]. When we are grown up, we speak constructive words so that we are able to do constructive things that will effect changes in different facets of our lives. Yes! The standard of our lives appreciates, when the foundation of our language skill appreciates.

Let see how the word of God helps us to develop strong reliance on the word as a source of faith in the voice of God.

---

[18] 1 Corinthians 13:11

Chapter Six

THE WORK OF THE WORD

The scripture is inspired by God. As Rick Renne will put it, "God breathe in human words." The word of God remains the only source to hear from God. It can grow into visions, audible voice, dreams, trance, prophetic utterances, and many more channels, His sovereignty will choose, however, it will reflect His character as revealed by the written word[19]

So, it is safe to say, every breakthrough a believer has achieved will be traced to a *word* from the Lord, and prospectively, every awaiting breakthrough needs to base its expectation on the *word* for manifestation.

The centurion in the Roman army who came to Jesus for the healing of one of his trusted servants, said

---

[19] 2 Peter 1:20-21

Jesus, "Send the *word only.*[20]" Behold, he got his servant healed through His *word*. It is the ability to hear a *word* that changes the circumstances, not the laying on of hands or the shouting in prayer but a *word* sent and an ear that receives.

My wife and I went through a stormy start in our marriage life. The first two months into our marriage, it was discovered that she had a full-blown cyst by the side of her ovaries which needed immediate surgery. She never had any pain before or felt any sort of cyst. It came as a shock to us because we were still on our honeymoon. And by the way, we are still there, and we have no plans of leaving.

We were very uncomfortable about the surgery, but the doctors warned us about what serious damage a rupture could cause to her.

We prayed but did not have the time to listen to the Spirit of God. And we had an emergency counselling, and our desperation overpowered our hearing of faith. Since we had only a few days to respond to the doctor, we were distracted with no patience to receive a word from the Lord.

So, we agreed on the operation to be performed. The night before the operation, we received a *word* that her ovaries will be saved, contrary to the doctor's speculation. The doctor had earlier reckoned she would have

---

[20] Luke 7:7 (BBE)

to lose her ovaries because of the size of the cyst. To God be the glory, the operation was successful!

> The dead things hear the word

Now here is the difference in receiving a word. Following the operation, we had further surprises. It took six months for her to recover as the cut was very deep. But the enemy was not done! At the ninth month into her recovery stage, we discovered yet another cyst which the doctor thought had the same size as the previous one. This time my wife went before the Lord. In one of those meetings, she got a word with God promising total healing.

Prophetic Word)* Psalm 107:20...*He sendeth his word, and healeth them, and delivereth them from their destructions.

Of course, this era is for the hearers. That same morning, after we believed the word we had received, as we got ready for church service, she felt a rumbling sensation and threw up some awful substance, and since then, she had not had any pain whatsoever. The doctors themselves ask, "What did you do?" Yes! We got the *word*!

The Scripture says that the *Word* became flesh. It is the work of the *word* to affect the earthly realms. It was the same word that worked tirelessly to shape and frame the universe[21]. The *word* from the Lord is

---

[21] Hebrew 11:3

the worker of miracles, and it says '...*He sent His word and healed them and delivered them from destruction.*[22] Excuse me for repetition, but it is worth it. In our days, many are trying to minimize the strength of the word of God, but His word will only get stronger and, in the end, overcome all system and structure in the world[23].

What have we heard all this time? The Lord has been speaking good things all these times. Can you not hear them from His word? They are for healing and deliverance and much more. Even the dead things in life can hear the Word and come to life.[24]

Young people are being drowned by music and alien noises today, having little to do with the essence of living. There are many missing the opportunity to encounter what we are really made from.[25] By disrupting the flow of the voice of God, many are thrown into the quagmire of confusion and a Life of just chasing dreams and shadows. Instead of going for the words of God, meant to heal, save, and deliver people from death.

Hebrews 4:12...*For the word of God is quick, and powerful, and sharper than any two-edged sword, piercing even to the dividing asunder of soul and*

---

[22] 4 Psalm 107:20
[23] Daniel 2:45
[24] John 5:25
[25] Genesis 1:26-28

spirit, and of the joints and marrow, and is a discerner of the thoughts and intents of the heart.
(KJV)

In this book, the Spirit is showing how in the last times, the events, the catastrophes, and the blessings would all be wrapped up in the sounds of the heavens, the sounds of the air, the sounds of the earth, and the sounds of man.

We cannot just walk away thinking that we are saved and will be blessed by the Lord. We need to understand that sound is a culture of heaven as well as of the earth and that we are wrapped in it in one way or the other. Sounds will be amazingly utilized in the episode that will bring about the last of days.

The next chapter "Four Great Signs" shows the magnitude and urgency that the Lord's voice wants to speak to us. How much will you speak if you know everything, how much compassion will you show when you feel everything, how much passion will you demonstrate if you sense everything, how much love will you give to all when your whole being is love? God is speaking by the Spirit with a loud voice today the same way as He spoke at the Tomb of Lazarus[26]

"Church, open your ears to Me, do not close the gates which is to receive the last time messages. I will speak in an open manner, and you will hear Me. My word

[26] John 11:43

shall become mighty in you. No weapon formed in the last time shall stand against you. Your ears are Mine; I want you to speak My word to the Bartimaeus, the Lazarus, the centurions in your days. The wind wants to hear My word and the seas want instruction, my people open your ears!"

Chapter Seven

FOUR GREAT SIGNS

The book of Revelation opens up with John, the Apostle of Jesus Christ, being banished to the island of Patmos by Roman officials who were bent on destroying the influence of the Gospel. How naïve can a nation or a people appear, to think that it is possible to kill an immortal God or silence His servants!

These four great phenomena are revealed in the book of Revelation, the book of profound value and full of the images and symbols of God's intentions and inter-actions for the safety and well-being of all mankind.

John settled in this wilderness with wild beasts on every side. Geographically, Patmos was a mining set-tlement, where roman prisoners were sent to serve out their prison term with hard labour. It is known that prisoners make it back from the hard labour mixed with poor sanitation and polluted air quality. Yet it was in these deplorable conditions where John was, and he could still connect with the voice of God. The Scripture says that he was in the spirit on the Lord's day, and there he saw the Lord Jesus Christ in splendour and glory.

Rev 1: 12-16... *And I turned to see the voice that spake with me.*
And being turned, I saw seven golden candlesticks;
And in the midst of these seven golden candlesticks
One like the unto the Son of man, clothed with a garment
Down to the foot, and girt about the paps with a golden girdle. His head and his hairs were white like wool, as
White as snow; and his eyes were as flame of fire. And
His feet like unto fine brass, as if they burned in a furnace;
And his voice as of many water. And he had in his right
Hand seven stars and out his mouth went a sharp two
Edged sword; and his countenance was as the sun shineth
In his strength. (KJV)

As the vision continued, John could not handle it anymore, and he fell, in his own word 'as dead.' Then,

Jesus began to reveal to John the mysteries concerning the church and the last days. One of those last days' signs is the seven stars and the seven candlesticks. Seven is the number of God, meaning perfection. The seven stars depict the seven angels of the church of God. Stressing His perfect and complete control over the church, and the seven candlesticks are the seven churches which shine as the light of the world.

To these seven churches did the Lord sent messages and they also depict the perfection of the church which would mean that the church is perfect but made up of imperfect men and women; thus, the messages to the church to bring them into perfection, of which position the church is now. After these things, he heard a voice saying, *'Come up hither.'*

Revelation 4:1... *After this I looked, and, behold, a door was opened in heaven: and the first voice which I heard was as it were of a trumpet talking with me; which said, Come up hither, and I will shew thee things which must be hereafter* (KJV)

Afterwards, we are open to realms where we can observe from God's perspectives; the God-view of earthly events in a different light. This is where we are taking up with John, to teach us how to perceive what was, is, and is to come. Again, the first voice that John had turned around to see, spoke to him again, and this time the invitation was to come up to a higher dimension.

– *'a trumpet was talking to me.'* It might be a bit strange of a term to describe the sound of a trumpet, however, this was his first introduction into the culture of heaven. Heaven operates in a speaking-through-sound-culture. Musicians actually would tell you that they think musically; thoughts are formed eventually in words.

> Every person in life is simply a product of sound

Music is not only a sound for a certain gender, age, or race, but for all. We are all musical; we eat and drink musically. We walk musically. Every person's stride differs and thus plays his or her own music when he or she walks.

Life-changing leaders or leadership are people or establishments' who have mastered their own style of music and sound culture. Every person, community, or nation are simply a product of sound culture they create.

Sound is the barrel that we all walk in and make different music out of. Sad to say, a lot of us dance to music as it were, but we never have a part in the creation of such. No wonder we serve God. For many, it is so impersonal, and they struggle with rightfully living. This is largely due to living on second hand sounds. They are not able to hear God for themselves, and so they walk and dance to corrupted sounds.

Every sound carries a soul, mostly the soul of a personality that is behind the scene. Meanings of different sounds can be derived only through the interpretation of the heart of the personality producing the sound. Could it be that John who placed his head on the chest of our Lord, still heard the need to be behind the trumpet? John said, *'the voice which I heard was as it were of a trumpet talking with me.'* He heard this trumpet in earthly places, yet he understood that it was a call from heaven because the next verse says that John confessed *'Immediately I was in the spirit...*[27]*'*

These are the unseen realms which the mortal eyes cannot see. Here, the flesh and the blood cannot walk and survive. These are the realms of the angelic and the throne of the Highest, God. This is what the sound of the Lord will do to anyone who dares to listen.

These chapters bring us into the throne of God and the experience of worship around the throne. We almost hear from the pages of the Bible, *'the sound of music, the adoration and the ambience created by the twenty-four elders, clad in white robes, with reverence on their faces as they behold this awesome being on the throne...*[28]

As we approach the fifth chapter, the journey reveals how Jesus Christ our Lord and Saviour, as the Lamb slain before the foundation of the world. He steps up bravely to open the book of judgement placed upon the whole world.

---

[27] Revelation 4:2
[28] Revelation 4:3-8

The book of judgment was sealed with seven seals. The royal call was whoever opens the seal, the same one must be ready to carry upon him the sins of the world. So, Jesus did and was willing to pay the price for man to be saved.

Revelation 5:9...*And they sang a new song, saying, Thou art worthy to take the book, and to open the seals thereof: for thou wast slain, and hast redeemed us to God by thy blood out of every kindred, and tongue, and people, and nation* (KJV)

OPENING OF THE SEALS

The first seal revealed the conquering rider on a white horse with a bow in his hands who was unleashed to conquer the nations.

The second seal revealed the rider and his red horse; this horse cut off the peace from the earth. This rider provoked wars in and among nations, and men slay each other, showing the deep darkness of the human heart.

The third seal revealed the black horse and its rider; this horse is appointed as the judge of his time. He shall take hold of the scale of balance, and the nations will desire and demand justice from the establishments as never before. The rider was empowered, and the command was not to damage the oil and the wine, both, which are great symbols of the Holy Spirit and his just dealing with mankind. This depicts that the ways of God cannot be hinder nor destroy by any generation.

The fourth seal revealed the pale horse whose rider is death, and hell followed them. This fourth seal unleashed two symbiotic riders, operating as one deadly force. Death confirming the fruit to the evil ways of mankind and the hell showing the destination of all who enjoyed and compromised in evil "...And they were given authority *and* power over a fourth part of the earth to kill with the sword and with famine and with plague (pestilence, disease) and with wild beasts of the earth." Alarming in our days will be the release of strong pestilence across the nations; these are viruses that will appear and seem to defy the medical profession. Humanity is already experiencing the brunt of the over-exploitation of nature's resources, now many regions of the world are experience climatic challenging such as flooding, erosions, drought which results to famine in large areas of the world due to greed and self-centred living.

The fifth seal revealed the souls of all the saints that were slain for their stands on the word of God with Lord in heavens waiting area. The Lord will comfort them till the final ascension of their fellow brothers in faith: From the ascension of Christ Jesus, believers suffer many evils from aggressors of the faith, instigated by the devil fury: Yet in our days, it continues; such that issue as political correctness is the new assassin, unleashed to gag the voice of righteousness and right and descent Christian living. The saints were given white robes as they waited for the final ascension of the rests.

The sixth seal was broken, and we see the unveiling of strong delusion. The earth will be shaking in such a vehement manner that the very centre of man's confidence will be totally disrupted. This is the effect of the dimensions of earthquake to which we shall look into this phenomenon more closely in chapter ten.

However, the sixth seal reveals the total failure in the systems of mankind trusts and introduces a great earthquake that shook the economies[29] of the world as we know it, we shall see more into the revelation of earthquake in chapter ten. The sun becoming black, is a revelation of confusion and lack of solution which will lead to the desperation of mankind. It triggers the moon to become red like blood signifying that mankind will not turn to the Lord for answers and help, this rebellion will not lead them into a time to recline and rest, instead it will be a time to fear and worry because of the unknown. Stars from the earthly perspective will represent the best of the society; meaning the best minds, in creativity, in innovation, in business, in governance, and in all works of life; they will all fall to

---

[29] Revelation 6:15

the earth. This darkening represents the days where humanity will not find rest in what usually causes rest. A whole region will be attacked by the spirit of restlessness, and this is a period where the church will become more pronounce and influential in the earthly realms.[30]

---

[30] Isaiah 2:2-4

Chapter Eight

THE SEVENTH SEAL

I will take more time in elaborating the seventh seal due to the fact that most of the revelation surrounding this book stems from the seventh seal.

Sounds of the trumpet lead the way in the opening of the seventh seal. You must see the significance of the seventh seal, how, for the first time in the book of Revelation, we read about silence in heaven, you could hear a pin drop. Apostle John describes how this silence matured to cover *"about the space of half an hour"*[31] as it were, a solemn ceremony to open the seventh seal such as was not the case for the other seals.

It is only the seventh seal among the others, which not only by silence but with seven angelic presence to usher these great mysteries. They were hand-picked or

---

[31] Revelation 8:1 BBE

47

employed to usher in the events which were ready to be unleashed from the seventh seal. This is the only seal with a far more widespread influence and reach than the others. It is also the only seal that is empowered to spread through seven dispensations as the Lord sees fit.

We must understand the brevity of the time that we have to accomplish what the Spirit of the Lord desires for the Church. From world events according to news media, we hear of more calamities, wars, and conflicts at a catastrophic level never dreamt would ever happen. As spirit filled believers, we must know by now that we are walking within the capsule of the seventh seal.

As Paul prayed for the eyes of the Ephesian church to be enlightened[32], I pray for the ear of this present-day church to be opened to the Word of the Lord.

It was at the seventh seal that the Lord spoke to me and continues to do expressly. Please try to understand what I am trying to convey to you; understand the times, and hear what the angelic trumpet is bringing into light. He spoke about the combination of voices and personalities that will bring in powerful manifestations and message for this age.

Vision is not made up of still or moving pictures or events, but they are voices encrypted. It must be

---

[32] Ephesians 1:17

decoded, unravelled, and understood. With His voice, He paints pictures and causes certain events, to take place in or around us, in a bid to transmit His vision and assignment to mankind. The more we hold a deaf ear against His instructions, the more intense the messages will resound.

God is a God of vision, and He will not create anything without a certain level's sound words. Hence a good number of well-meaning Christians will favour themselves to see and run with divine visions with deafness or very little hearing ability, how frustrating could this become?

The Prophets from the Old Testament show us how it is done: Isaiah said... 'the *word* that Isaiah the son of Amoz *saw*[33] concerning Judah and Jerusalem. ...the *words* of Amos... which he *saw*[34], confirming that we must, first of all, become great audionaries in other to be great visionaries. There is no place for deafness in the kingdom.

These men captured what they saw through their ear gates. In these last days, the enemy is succeeding in many quarters to hinder or deceive the believer in the area of sight because we have neglected the revelation of hearing from the Lord.

---

[33] Isaiah 2:1
[34] Amos 1:1

From the eighth to the twenty first chapter in the book of Revelation, we capture the various sounds and hear the noise of activities after this great silence, as the entire heavens erupted with sounds that they were familiar to heavenly creatures, but this time it carried more; it was the force of sounds and the uproar of waves that followed that triggers the beginning of great things.

These angels who will blow the trumpet of the Lord were strategically positioned to influence with sound and bring the systems to align with the desires of God for his creation. These sounds were going to be the sounds of judgment and chaos, woe and calamity, and more importantly, of opportunities, of blessing and abundance.

These Four Great Signs in the earth are God's design to keep His people on top of the world, so long as we perceive by hearing the events that are taking place. Most breakthroughs are going to be by someone who heard something. Leading by hearing will take on a whole new level.

Elijah among a few was such a man, who was led by hearing. He was able to depose Jezebel who by demonic powers, controlled the entire geopolitical, economic, and religious realms of Israel in her days. Somehow, she had gained access to the highest position in Israel and introduced strange and demonic systems, which led the king and the whole nation astray.

Elijah came on the scene like a thunderbolt from God.[35] By the word of the Lord, he went straight to the king's palace and began to challenge the powers that be. God used him mightily to bring the people back to the saving knowledge of the kingdom of God.

The height of spiritual warfare is when the people of God can, by the power of God, command nature to serve the purpose of God on earth. Elijah did just so. He shut up the heavens and commanded no rain to fall for a period of three years.

But why is he such a leader? Because when you carry out a study on the activities of Elijah, you never see him seeing a vision, rather you hear "the word of the Lord" coming to Elijah.

He displayed tremendous power.[36] The Old Testament showed him as one with an elevated level of hearing and listening that set him apart from the rest. The most profound demonstration of the power of God was when he confronted the Baal worshippers on the mount of Carmel. At the end of that confrontation, Gods favour backed up Elijah while he prayed, fire from the Lord fall down and consumed the burnt offering and licked up the waters[37], after which he ordered the destruction of the demonic priests.

---

[35] 1 King 17:1
[36] James 5:17-19
[37] 1 King 18:38

Elijah furthers displayed his audionary qualities when he heard the sound of rain. He could perceive that the showers were going to be heavy. As he then declared *'for there is sound of abundance of rain.'* [38] and this was ever before his servant could see the formation of rain clouds.

It was the power of hearing that brought Elijah back from the realms of fatigue and depression[39]. As he ran for his life and hid in a cave in the mountains, it was *the still small voice* that came to his rescue. Can you hear that sound? Can you hear the rush, like Elijah, who exclaims to the King Ahab "...*get up, eat and drink for there are sounds of abundance of rain"? There is a sound!*

Visionary would soon be empowered by 'Audionaries' (this word I made up here). The world would catch up to this, if or when God's people believe Him. Why? God would always come to the believer first before turning to the kings on earthly place to reveal a dispensational mystery. God only does that when His people pay Him no attention. God revealed the world famine to Pharaoh. He also revealed the world governmental structure that would come into existence to Nebuchadnezzar. Cyrus was anointed by God to aid the releases of the Jewish nation from captivity to go and build the beloved Promised Land.

---

[38] 1 Kings 18:41 BBE
[39] **1 King 19:12-13**

Jesus demanded that we moved in these audio-visual dimensions proficiently when He speaks to us. He points out in

Mark 8:18...*Having eyes, see ye not? and having ears, hear ye not? and do ye not remember?*

These are questions in which Jesus was pulling them into the revelation of the visionary and the audionary.

Jesus himself demonstrated great works by operating on these two forms of leadership in His ministry when He first said …

John 5:19… *Then answered Jesus and said unto them, Verily, verily, I say unto you, The Son can do nothing of himself, but what he seeth the Father do: for what things soever he doeth, these also doeth the Son likewise.*

20 For the Father loveth the Son, and sheweth him all things that himself doeth: and he will shew him greater works than these, that ye may marvel. (KJV)

And secondly, in a later chapter, He describes receiving by hearing. Notice how He connected hearing to the ability of speaking words, how the Father gave Him commandment! These are words received by auditory means but now converted to power supply...

John 12:49... *For I have not spoken of myself; but the Father which sent me, he gave me a commandment, what I should say, and what I should speak.*

50 And I know that his commandment is life everlasting: whatsoever I speak therefore, even as the Father said unto me, so I speak. (KJV)

Voices, thundering, lightning, and earthquake are these great signs and sounds which have been released into earthly places to warn of the onslaughts of the enemy on the mind of the people of the earth. These I will be treating in the chapters to follow. They are defences against the enemy's strategies. They are feeders and great informants to the people of God on divine waves of protection and warnings, and the demonstration of God's love.

The sounds of destruction that the enemy is unleashing into the world today are only a distraction from the real revelations that God has in store for the world. Believers are now understanding the significance of our times and getting to speed with it and should not to be lackadaisical about what they hear and sense. But this is the time where we need to stretch face down on the golden altar of righteousness and cry out for the lost souls of many and also for the refreshing of the saints.

The elements of the sound are taking centre stage in the secular world and are catching up like wildfire.

Our young people are being sucked away from life like dust into the vacuum. The reason being, the enemy has seen the transition, and his intentions are to endeavour to create a conflict, to cause a noise barrier to hinder the hearing of the authentic sound of God.

But he is too late as usual! God is already causing some people to hear some powerful word that is changing entire regions of the world with the power of revelation knowledge, sign, and wonders.

The word is, *'Change the atmosphere of the devil, in your homes, in your schools, and in your business affairs. Create an atmosphere where he cannot operate and cause confusion.'*

There is a real and persistent danger, and we are going to see more disasters of epic proportions around the world, if we do not increase the volume of righteousness in our lives. The natural disasters that we see and the widening of the circumference of these great signs are actually sent to bless the world but rather being destructive because they can only be constructive when righteousness reigns.

Chapter Nine

VOICES
Thundering - Lightening - Earthquake

What are these elements composed of? We are faced with the last plagues of destructions, a loveless world, wickedness, haters of God, and the synchronisation of the worship of Man.

These sounds seem to be on the increase, but God in His sovereignty knows how much power He has in store for us in these last times; He produced in His kingdom the weapon of sound, which would be distinctive and instructive to the nations. And to His children, He is saying *'if any has ear let him hear.'*

The creation of these elements is seen clearly in the third to fifth verses in the eighth chapter of the book of Revelation.

Rev.8:3-5...*and another angel came and stood by the altar, having a golden censer; and there was given unto him much incense, that he should offer it with the prayers of all saints upon the golden altar which was before the throne. And smoke of the incense, which came the prayer of the saints ascended up before God out of the angel's hand. And the angel took the censer, and filled it with the fire of the altar, and cast it into the earth: and there were voices, and thunderings, and lightnings and an earthquake.* (KJV)

These mighty angelic beings stood in ready position to announce great things, of not only such things that have passed, but things that will occur in present times and for the future.

These voices, thunderings, lightnings, and earthquakes messengers are already here. We shall go in-depth and bring out the meaning of these great messengers. Before that, we must experience that these are sounds of the last days; these are messengers and informants to the world and the believers.

They are the enlighteners of the worshippers; they are to humble proud men. They are the answers to the cry of the righteous. They will swallow the encroaching enemy; they warn of the impending doom. They are music to the ears of the saved and death to the condemned by choice, because nobody has to be on the side of the condemned. Jesus has paid the entire price for all those who seek His salvation.

Yes! Jesus was speaking of the last days:

Luke 21: 8-11... *"Take heed that you are not deceived: for many shall come in my name, saying I am the Christ; and the time draweth near: go ye not therefore after them, But when ye shall hear of wars and commotion, be not terrified: for these things must first come to pass: but the end is not by and by." He also said to them, "Nation shall rise against nation, and kingdom against kingdom: And great earthquakes shall be in diverse places, and famine, and pestilences, and fearful sights and great signs shall there be from the heavens."* (KJV)

PROPHETIC PREPAREDNESS

Revelation 8:4... *And the smoke of the incense, which came with the prayers of the saints, ascended up before God out of the angel's hand.* (KJV)

These great sounds have been made possible by divine preparedness and human participation. If we are ready to witness the supernatural, we are to know that there is a need for prophetic preparedness in the spirit, expressed through our prayerfulness.

Why are we hard of hearing these days? It is simply because we do not know how to enter into this realm of preparedness. Remember, earlier we mentioned a few men who left undeniable proof of God's grace on their lives. They were saints like you and I, but the one difference might be that they prayed on the golden altar before the Lord '...*that he should offer it with the prayers of all saints upon the golden altar which was before the throne.'* This means that they prayed on the plateau of righteousness before the Lord.

Thank God for the cloud of witnesses who have prayed! What are we doing to make the church know this? Yes! We need to send up our part of prayers so that the next generation may be consumed with the *sound* from the Lord.

We need to snatch people from the jaws of Satan and his demons. We are called to rip apart and destroy the kingdom of devils and destroy their high places with the *sound* of heaven.

It was the *sound* from heaven that brought down the Jericho walls![40] It was the sound of heaven that made the steps of four lepers from Samaria sound like the matching of a great army![41] Your size or age does not matter! Let your prayers go up! You are called by God! You are the righteousness of God in Christ Jesus! Now,

---

[40] Joshua 6:1-27
[41] 2 King 7:3-20

it is time to release the *sound of righteousness* to confound the wicked, to swallow up the unrighteous work of the devil, and to set the captives free!

Joshua 6:20... *So the people shouted when the priests blew with the trumpets: and it came to pass, when the people heard the sound of the trumpet, and the people shouted with a great shout, that the wall fell down flat, so that the people went up into the city, every man straight before him, and they took the city.*(KJV)

2 Kings 7:6...*For the Lord had made the host of the Syrians to hear a noise of chariots, and a noise of horses, even the noise of a great host: and they said one to another, Lo, the king of Israel hath hired against us the kings of the Hittites, and the kings of the Egyptians, to come upon us.* (KJV)

Chapter Ten

EARTHQUAKES
The Sign of Bewilderment

Revelation 11:13...*and the same hour was a great earthquake, and the tenth part of the city fell, and in the earthquake was slain of men seven thousand: and the remnant were affrighted, and gave glory to God of heaven.* (KJV)

The first of these great signs I wish to discuss, not in their order but by choice, is earthquakes.

And the angel took the censer, and filled it with the fire of the altar (prayers of the saint), and cast it into the earth: and there were voices, and thundering, and lightnings and an earthquake[42].

---

[42] Revelation 8: 5

I want to be able to conclude that nothing simply happens by chance. All earthly signs have supernatural origin. One of the creative sounds the Lord has given to the believer to affect both his personal life and world events and to enforce the order of the Kingdom of God is the sign called 'earthquakes.'

In the book of Revelation, earthquakes did not get introduced until the prayers of the saints were offered mix with the incense from the Lord which burnt on His golden altar.

This is very significant, because some people may be shocked or surprised to know that the origin of earthquakes is spiritual. We are always drawn to the physical destruction it causes, to lives and properties. We do mourn victims of their loved once as our hearts sympathize with them. However, in recent times, we experience the rise of these natural disasters, and as the scripture forth tells it, it will only get higher as humanity neglects its spirituality.

While the pains are real, there is a spiritual side which the world need consultation on.

EARTHQUAKE ARE SPIRITUAL

Earthquakes are spiritual because it was in the spiritual realms that John saw their origin, and as we do trace the role of this member of the great family of sounds, we see a unique picture of its role in these last days.

The seventh seal phase reveals the earth and the church's prophetic time clock of our times.

When all the other seals were opened, the events unfolded without such spiritual protocol as we will experience at the seventh. The opening of the seventh seal was well orchestrated by the Lord. This particular seal is for the church to see the power and strength endowed to her in these end times. The church needs to hear from this great messenger and learn from its prompting before they ever enter the earthly realms.

According to the book of Revelation, earthquakes went forward before any other catastrophes came through to the realms of the earth. From the Scriptural point of view, earthquakes, or any of the other signs in question are not evil because they also take place in the presence of God.

Revelation 11:19...*and the temple of God was opened in heaven, and there was seen in his temple the ark of his testimony: and there were lightnings and voices, and thundering, and an earthquake, and great hail stone.*

The only difference is that, when these signs take place in the earthly realms, due to the unrighteous found in the earth, it cannot stand the order that the earthquake desires to bring. Hence the experience of disasters we see around us. Earthquakes are going to be used more in our days to cause men to design God's ordained order. The system of the world will give way for the life of God to be birth in the heart of mankind for compassion for humanity.

GODS CHOSEN SYSTEM.

John had seen the first angel blowing the first trumpet and how these sounds went on till the seventh angel opened the seal. We read as these sounds went out, disasters began to take place in diverse places on the earth and in the spirit. As John describes these disasters and woes, he stops and lets the reader see what was going on at the backdrop of each world's events, which seems to be taking place simultaneously.

In the eleventh chapter of the book of Revelation, John stopped to show us two personalities that were sent by God to bring a message from the Lord. They were called two olive trees, representing the symbiotic relationship of the Apostolic and the prophetic anointing of the Lord's church of the last days.[43]

This is another study entirely. Our focus is on the effect of their ministry and how unchallenged they were, until they accomplished their assignments and

---

[43] Revelation 11:4

64

how nature worked with them in accomplishing such great work.

In spite of all their works of great power, the enemy still tried to kill them and even succeeded to put them to death for a moment and introduce his own style of leadership, causing people everywhere to mock God's style of leadership while the people laugh at the bodies of these two prophets, which lay dead on the ground where our Lord was crucified[44]

The world will always find the opportunity to try to belittle God's chosen system and celebrate the death of a system which is God-filled. Does this sound familiar? The world could not wait to mock you as soon as you become a believer; to mock your faith[45]. They jump down your throat to strangle the life of God out of you, once they find out where your faith lies. Nevertheless, it didn't change your testimony that God is good, faithful, and true. And, surely, He still fights for you.

These two great prophets of God lay down there for three days. Now, the Bible tells how, on the third day, the life of God came into these two olive tree personalities, and a voice from heaven called them up out of the system that mocked them. What happened next was the role of the earthquake![46]

---

[44] Revelation 11:8-9
[45] Revelations 11:10
[46] Revelation11:13

The earthquake became the final sign that turns men's heart to God[47]. Earthquake is designed by God and takes on a new light when we see its (earthquake) dynamic move in the spirit realm: How it disorganises the worldly belief systems and goes on boldly to test the worthless foundations of the world's principles and standards. It is always successful in the spirit to pull them down and to establish the kingdom of God's principles and precepts.

It never ceases to amaze me how the earthly kingdom will forget her poor and dying in different parts of the globe. Not until the earth opens up with fury, then their ears and eyes open.

It takes an earthquake to destabilize one region of the earth to expose their plight of another part. After such devastation, will the media, aid organisations, and governments turn to attend to the needs and plights of a once forgetting region where the poor and dying have been suffering for a long time.

As believers, our eyes need not experience these surprises before we wake up to the call of spiritual effects here on earth before we move. Our move will create righteousness ever before this heavenly sign, the earthquake, reaches the earthly realms.

Earthquakes not only help to destabilize worldly systems and governments, but also to swallow up the

---

[47] Revelation 11:13

encroachment of Satan's attacks and his assigned agents.

As John went deeper in the spirit realms, he saw the events that unfolded when Jesus, the Word, was about to be made flesh and how the enemy battled to kill his earthly mother of Jesus, Mary[48].

EARTHQUAKE THE HELPER

John shows us from chapter twelve onwards, how Satan was kicked out of heaven by force and how the angels who sided with him to fight the holy angels fell out of the Heavens. God's plan still was to create man, to let him have dominion over the earthly places, because Satan did not like this idea, he began to wage another battle against the Redeemer who had been announced.

Revelation 12:10...*And I heard a loud voice saying in heaven, now is come the salvation, and strength, and the kingdom of our God, and the power of his Christ: for the accuser of our brethren is cast down, which accused them before our God day and night.* (KJV)

With the determination to terminate the pregnancy of Mary, a demonic law instigated by satan was passed by Caesar Augustus, which warranted all people must

---

[48] Revelation 12:16

go to their hometown and register their names for census. The pregnant Mary rode on a donkey for between 85 – 90 miles (126 kilometres) "It was a fairly gruelling trip," said Strange, who annually leads an excavation team at the ancient city of Sepphoris, near Nazareth. Research shows, it would have been long and cold for any pregnant woman nearing full term to sustain their baby yet, God protected her from miscarriage till they reached Bethlehem.

The enemy did not stop his onslaught, in that while Jesus was now a baby, he stirred envy in the heart of King Herold to murder. He orders every male from two years and under[49] to be put to death by the sword. Herod's attack was so great on both the mother and child, that John saw it in the spirit[50] ...*And to the woman were given two wings of a great eagle, that she might fly into the wilderness, into her place, where she is nourished for a time, and times, and half a time, from the face of the serpent*[51].

Prompted by the angel of The Lord, Joseph and Mary fled into the wilderness with baby Jesus because of the gruesome order. In the spirit, John saw this event as the great flood which came out of the mouth of the dragon. That old serpent the devil, sent to destroy the woman, but God used, earthquake as the great helper of the woman.

---

[49] Matthew 2:16-18

[50]

[51] Revelation 12:14

Revelation 12:16...*And the earth helped the woman, and the earth opened her mouth and swallowed up the flood which the dragon cast out of his mouth.* (KJV)

There are floods of the enemy against your family, churches, business concerns, and nations, design for great destruction of both life and properties. We need to have an ear of the spirit to discern before they happen, so that you are able to position yourself to gain victory over them. Governments and high authorities over regions must employ the help of intercessors, to become eyes and ears for their nations at these times. To govern the spirit realms for maximum defence against the last onslaught of the enemy.

These days, we see the floods of war, hunger, sickness, strange viruses' disintegration of families, pestilences, and continuous widening of the gap between the poor and the rich in most parts of the world. These are all evil floods in the spirit realms, and only the hearer-leaders can stand and command the earth to swallow up these things in our times

Visionaries are vital, but where are the new breed of 'Audionaries'? They will hear great sound from the spirit and become bold to declare it. We are God's first response team, to hear the seismic sounds in the spirit, before they occur and use the weapon of sound that God has sent to us, to our advantage.

There are going to be great shaking through the globe like never before. These shaking is to show the world leaders the futility of governance without God (through Jesus Christ) and without the guidance of the Holy Spirit.

TWO SYSTEMs

God-sounds are positioned across the globe right now and are being proclaimed like in the days of Uzziah, the King of Israel, when an earthquake swept across the land and brought an end to tyranny and molestation, both spiritual and physical.

Just as God warned Ariel (another name for Jerusalem), the city where David dwelt in the same manner … **Isaiah 29:6**… ***Thou shalt be visited of the Lord of Hosts with thunder, and with earthquake, and great noise, with storms and tempest, and the flame of devouring fire.*** KJV

Earthquake is designed to bring balance in the government of man by enforcing righteousness in the lands of the people of God. Earthquake signifies the destabilisation of the governmental systems of the world, by exposing their weaknesses and their unlawfulness habits. It will expose shady operations, false promises, and their inability to deliver. By reason of earthquake, the establishments of the world will lose their grip on the mind of the masses, who may have once trusted their boosting's, sparking a new search for the living God.

In the Scriptures, we see the Lord using earthquakes at all times to bring down one system and to raise up another; empowering the expanse of one kingdom and overthrow of the other.

God sometimes uses earthquakes to separate His anointed ones from the self- appointed. A good example was the case of Moses in the wilderness when he was faced with the rebellion engineered by Korah[52]. He led a band of chiefs to question Moses' authority. God had chosen and anointed Moses to lead His people out of Egypt and to bring them to the land of Canaan.

In our days, man's standard in judging good name and reputation has crept into the Church. Whereby we talk about superstars and celebrities, even much more than the faithful kingdom builders. We even give ourselves awards and receiving awards, but we must not lose sight of God-ordained systems of promotion. God does not look on outward appearances but at heart[53]. The end does not always justify the means, as we are made to believe today. God still has a higher vetting standard.

Moses' system was God-ordained, but Korah and his band of "good men" will be frustrated as they try to pull

---

[52] Number 16:1-2
[53] 1 Samuel 16:7

down the GOD system of choice. The world will fight to break God-system by employing good name and reputable men by worldly standards, but the shaking has long begun, and it is escalating, both in the church and the world.

Disasters are getting ready to be experienced because "Korah" and his band of men will be relentless in their aim to fix their 'GOOD system' and put down the God system, but a sure sign is emerging in the heavenly place to vindicate those standing in righteousness. God became so displeased with this group that, in the end, an earthquake became an instrument to swallow up the intentions of the enemy. Thus, God vindicated His man.[54]

---

[54] Numbers 16:1-33

Chapter Eleven

LIGHTNINGS
The Sign of Judgement

Revelation 8:5...*And the angel took the censer, and filled it with the fire of the altar, and cast it into the earth: and there were voices, and thunderings, and lightnings and an earthquake.*(KJV)

Lightning was mentioned as one of these four Great signs of the heavens and earth. Its full strength was seen when another angel was introduced in the midst of all the great chaos on the earth. [55]

When God introduces lightning as one of the sounds of the times, He is sending us the sounds of judgments on the worldly systems, and whenever judgment is passed, there has to be an enforcer of the judgment.

---

[55] Revelation 18:1-2

In any judgment procedure, there must also be benefactors that rejoice after all is said and done.

The church must align herself as God enforcers and be the benefactor of this current move of the Spirit. Audionaries will be the only calibre of leaders that can enforce Godly principles in our days. They are able to create such force that will unleash shape judgement against systems promoting satanic agenda. This will manifest in the service industries, hospitality industries, fashion, and cosmetic industries.

There will be great embarrassment that will hit the worldly scene to fight radically against the self-centred habits and the greedy establishments that are retaining values meant for humanitarian purposes.

SOUNDS OF EMBARRASSMENT

Psalms 18:14...*Yea, he sent out his arrows, and scattered them; and he shot out lightnings, and discomfited them*. (KJV)

The world's hunger for unity without God is growing. The rise of Social media and its great influence in recent times speaks clearly of this great hunger to gather under one umbrella of philosophy and so-called spiritualism.

In the midst of this hunger lies a grave and growing discomfort. Privacy violation, criminal activities, identity theft, child molestations, and loneliness just to mention that goes on behind the freedom and political correctness, but these are signs of this discomfort. Any gathering not of God presents an arena for the enemy to deceive and establish his false systems.

Lightening is God's power to embarrass the power of the enemy. People who have trained their ears to hear, do know that when judgment is passed on any situation, that could spell an end to certain collaborations or industries that lack divine direction.

There are companies we see now as formidable and which we assume will be affected by the tide of recession, but they will be shut down within a day because it will time to embarrass their ungodly activities and they will be taking over by individuals that are willing to see the move of God for the restoration of God agendas.

Revelation 18:10...*Standing afar off for the fear of her torment, saying, Alas, alas, that great city Babylon, that mighty city! For in one hour is thy judgment come.* (KJV).

Babylon here signifies the highest earthly system that ever existed, great in economic strength and political power. It was known as the golden kingdom. God showed Nebuchadnezzar through his dream, and by Daniel's interpretation, his kingdom was the golden era of all worldly systems and how no other kingdom system on earth could attain such eminence as the Babylonians did. Yet, they were humbled and embarrassed in a day[56]!

Lightnings are sound waves that convey the flashes of the anger of heaven to destroy the works of the kingdom of darkness. In the eighteenth chapter of the book of Revelation, God began to state the sins of the systems of the world and their pride and conceit. In the second verse, God stated… *"And he cried with a mighty voice saying Babylon the great is fallen, is fallen, and is become the habitation of devils, and the hold of every foul spirit, and caged of every unclean and hateful bird."*

Revelation 18:3…*For all nations have drunk of the wine of the wrath of her fornication, and the kings of the earth have committed fornication with her, and the merchants of the earth are waxed rich through the abundance of her delicacies.* (KJV)

'For all nations have drunk of the wine of the wrath' shows how all nations would have the same drive for power like the Babylonians did. Even in these days, we see nations pushing for weapons of war to be produced, and researches carried out to make them more dangerous. Behind all these is the stench of greed and pride, and the intoxicant called power. [57]

---

[56] Isaiah 45 / Revelations 8:18
[57] Revelation 8:18

The judgment here is to break down the unjust walls built by Satan and his cohorts. It is to frustrate the plans of the devil and to liberate the bound souls of men, setting the captives free.

God encourages the saints...*Rejoice over her, thou heaven, and ye holy apostles and prophets; for God hath avenged you on her.*[58]

WEALTH TRANSFER

Wealth is the total well fair of God lavished on His people[59] for the entire spirit soul and body[60] development. Lightning flashes in the dark (spiritual realms) to reveal the treasures that are meant for the believers and to help them retrieve their blessings[61]. The flash of lightning can be fast, but the hearer need not be concerned with where the lightning is going but with what it is carrying.

To the believer, God has destined a royal living, clothes of fine linen decked with gold and precious stones, where these can pass for physical riches. However, the most important side of the deal is when we can hear of these things in the spirit and have the satisfaction to wheel them in, in the physical.

---

[58] Revelation 18 : 20
[59] 1 John 3:1
[60] 1 Thessalonians 5:23
[61] Isaiah 43:3

As a result of the mystery of lightening, God shows us the judgment and the transfer of position and wealth. The Bible says in

Revelation 18:16-18....*And saying, Alas, alas, that great city, that was clothed in fine linen, and purple, and scarlet, and decked with gold and precious stone and pearls! For in one hour so great riches is come to nought. And every shipmaster, and all the company in ships, and sailors, and as many as trade by sea, stood afar of and cried when they saw the smoke of her burning, saying, what city is like unto this great city?* (KJV)

Lightning was that sound that God used to reveal the judgment pronounced against Babylon, this encapsulates all other systems that are of this world, to bankrupt the way they treat God's treasure. Such that as soon as Cyrus took over Babylon, God commanded and stirred up His spirit to released God children from bondage with great wealth, so that they can go and start rebuilding the temple and revive the state of Israel again.

May the Lord open our ears to understand His ways as we approach a time when the world will be experiencing a great trail of destruction, but on the other hand, the church will be experiencing powerful move of kingdom wealth to fund the kingdom.

May we step out as sons of God to enforce this judgment of God! We are here to bring out the true meaning of the lightning that will strike and also to bring God's hope, love, and mercy to many people and help them receive the saving knowledge of Christ.

Chapter Twelve

THUNDERING
The Call For Worship

The Church has been trained on how to pray for her needs and receive from God. She has also been taught the use of praying according to her desire and helped see how to use the invisible do the impossible.

In all these, do you hear the call to worship? Worship is the extreme end of all your service. Worship is the focus of all who want to live a godly life. Worship and the heart to worship God in spirit and in truth[62] may be one of the gems that the church needs to go back and dig for. Worship is why the Lord saved us.

Thundering is the God-sound in worship! It is the sound of the voices of worship! We need to hear worship

---

[62] John 4:23-24

before we can enter in and use this awesome sound of God!

The sound of worship thundering was used in the days of Joshua. The march around the Jericho wall signifies the groaning with words that cannot be uttered.

As they marched in silence, the prayers went up and mixed with the spices or the incense of heaven. At the right time, when God said 'Shout,' thank God for the 'audionary' leader Joshua, he heard it, the thunder of their voices went up to make way for God to cause an earthquake that ripped through the walls.

Joshua 6:20... *So the people shouted when the priests blew with the trumpets: and it came to pass, when the people heard the sound of the trumpet, and the people shouted with a great shout, that the wall fell down flat, so that the people went up into the city, every man straight before him, and they took the city. (KJV)*

HEAVEN ON EARTH

Worship is not just about beautiful voices or instruments! It has an impact on the soul that connects with God; it's the hearer of the sounds of heaven. Heaven worship and earth must access what is in heaven, so heavens worship can be super imposed on the earth[63].

---

[63] Matthew 16:19

It is the lifestyle that mirrors the divine; it is faith at its best. Worship is sweet and pleasant, yet it commands great terror in the camp of the enemy. It is the power for the supernatural to be poured on the natural. It is the believe and strength to sustain the presence of almighty.

The proud cannot worship, for they are self-centred and not God-centred. The deaf in spirit cannot worship because, after a while, they get frustrated. The unstable cannot worship because they would always waltz out of step.

WORSHIP NOW!

What a mighty weapon God has given to us! In the book of Revelation, *thundering* is mentioned four times and twice in the book of Exodus. At both times in Exodus, we see the *"thundering"* making the people submit themselves to the service of the Lord.

In **Exodus 9:28**, Pharaohs said, ***"Entreat the LORD (for it is enough) that there be no more mighty thundering and hail; and I will let you go, and ye shall stay no longer."***

Through *thundering*, God will break the grip of all kinds of pharaohs that hinder the movement of God's power for the supernatural amongst God people in Jesus' name!

In the last days, the sound of *thundering* would separate the true from the false worshippers. It is God's *thundering* that the hearer needs to hear in order to sing the right song today. Singing produces and sustains any culture, and to keep the culture of heaven prevalent, the church needs the songs of heaven.

A church that can hear this will never sing out of tune. The culture will be of power and not mere words and rhetoric. It is time for Heaven's culture to permeate all the realms of human establishments.[64] Thundering will elevate church to greater heights to accomplish great things for God in and around its neighbourhoods.

The business saint who chooses to hear the song of the times would never run out of ideas, concepts, and systems. The leader who chooses to hear the song of heaven would never lead with presumptions and assumptions, but there will be clarity that will bring greater manifestations.

Oh! What a tragedy when we sing and dance out of beat with God! Our spiritual ankles are strained, and we get so spiritually tired too quickly. Some, out of share frustration, will rely on the dangers of second hand information.

Exodus 20:18...*And all the people saw the thunderings, and the lightnings, and the noise of the*

---

[64] Matthew 6:10

trumpet and the mountain smoking: and when the people saw it, they removed, and stood afar off

The children of Israel settled for secondary hearing as the modern church/ believers are being tempted today. The dangers of secondary hearing will be discussed at length in 'Voices- Announcing the Kingdom', the next chapter. However, the children of Israel could not stand the noise and the thundering because they were not hearers; they have dwelt in the realms of sight for too long. That is where the church is at the moment; to see and get away. If we have the ear of the spirit, the tables are turning. *"...he who has ear, let him hear what the Spirit is saying to the church."*[65]

So, in the seventh seal, however, God introduces *thundering* as one of the messengers within this sound generation to speak to us about worship and the concentration on godly sound.

In the music world, for example, we are being drowned daily by sounds that are released by various artists around the globe. Earlier, it used to be the case that an album may take up to four years before a new one is released by the same artist. But these days, within a short period of four to six years, artists seem to be signing agreements to release three to five albums every year.

---

[65] Revelations 3:22

The demonic world has slowly caught up to know that God has given the church a more powerful tool to enter into thunderous worship. So, the (demonic system) is keen to increase the volume of their music.

In spite of this distraction, hearers in the spirit can discern and receive thunderous sound that will frighten the Pharaohs or to pull down the Jericho walls of our day.

Worship is a lifestyle that moves with the thundering of God. This passage of Scriptures takes us into the atmosphere of true thunderous worship described as if these voices were of a great multitude, the voice of many waters, and as the voice of mighty thundering, saying, *"Alleluia: for the Lord God omnipotent reigneth."*[66]

These thunderings declare God's omni potency. They display His all-powerful nature and His wondrous work. This is the reason why, when the Lord thunders from heaven, the enemies scatter[67], they cannot stand the praise of God's holy name. Worship is the life that experiences the all-powerful nature of God; His strength is manifested as we are carried along with these great thundering in the heavens.

Yes, there would be earthly manifestations; these thundering would rip through continents to demonstrate the power of the Almighty God. The nations will

---

[66] Revelation 19 :6
[67] Psalm 68:1

see and hear the roar of thundering that will separate the worshipper from the hypocrite.

New songs are signs from the thundering of the Lord. Often time in our ministries, we have received fresh ministry of new songs as we corporately worship in the spirit. These are captured by the ears of hearers (the audionary) and converted into power words, which will be heard by many, and that will turn around the course of history, around neighbourhood, churches, and towns and also in commerce.

Yes! The shift is beginning, and unbelievable things are about to take place. *'Where are My hearers and they that seek after Me' is the call of the heaven. Get your barn houses ready. Do not hold back when I say move; for production in all areas of life will take the pace of My thundering and hearers are bound to respond positively'.* The world will soon be shaken[68].

SECRET OF ABUNDANCE

These great *thundering* in the nineteenth chapter of the book of Revelation introduce us to the abundance that follows at the most important event in the history of heaven and earth, the Great Supper of the Lamb. This is a worshipful supper, where the Lamb is joined by His Bride. An atmosphere of joy and celebration! John said that when he saw these things, he fell at the

---

[68] Ecclesisates 12:13

angels' feet to worship the angel, but the angel stopped him and said, "No! Worship God."

Yes! Worship God with your heart, soul, and body. Love the Lord and worship Him with all of your being, releasing yourself into the surrendered mode in the everlasting arms of Jehovah. Worship God, this is the end of man.

The worship of God, the acknowledgement of His grace and mercy, His love and kindness, His patience and longsuffering. Worship His Majesty, the all-powerful, yet all condescending God. Worship and thundering reveal his abundant nature where all things exist, and without Him, there will be no life form; even man for it is for worship God made man.

This great thundering opened the veil to true worship, the worship of God and the Lamb. We then saw the Lord arrayed in gallant attire on a white horse with all the armies of heaven behind Him, ready to go out to take all the titles of the earthly kings by force and send their ring leader, the devil, into prison for a thousand years and resume His reign as the King of kings and the Lord of lords.

This thundering is stirring up individuals who God will use to speak in places the church least expects the name of Jesus to be called. The power of thundering will orchestrate the name of Jesus to be called in realms that will usually stamp out the name. The enemy cannot stop the name of Jesus. As the days draw to a close, the name of Jesus will be thundered to confound the enemy, and because Jesus will raise unpredictable men and woman around the globe, the church will receive masses free publicity that will, in the end, create very high visibility. They will be unassuming until the day of their manifestation.

Revelation 19:16.... *And he hath on his vesture and on his thigh a name is written, KING OF KINGS, AND LORD OF LORDS.* (KJV)

Chapter Thirteen

VOICES
Announcing the Kingdom

1 Corinthians 14:10...*There are, it may be, so many kinds of voices in the world, and none of them is without significance.* (KJV)

This is Apostle Paul writing to the Corinthians. This may seem obvious in the physical but carries a monumental significance in the realms of the spirit. Paul says that every voice has its own significance.

Significant means worthy of attention or noteworthy. Because every time we hear any voice after a time, it must certainly affect our thinking, and it will end up ordering our steps.

The significant of the voice is in the words. So, to be able to do significant things in the kingdom of God, we must hear from Him and let His word order our steps. The major hindrance around a modern-day Christian would be the presence of secondary voices.

Secondary voices are passed-on voices by secondary vehicle. Like in the game, Chinese whisper, where participants sit around a table and information is whispered into the ear of the first person to relay it to the next person, and they are expected to pass the same information silently around the table. On many occasions, the message would be distorted before it gets back to the original source. Similarly, it is very dangerous when we relate to God through secondary voices. Do you know the name of this game?

Secondary voice does not give room for relationships. It gives rise to familiarity. Nowadays, we have people who are hunting for a word in every meeting and end up frustrated. God is a personal God. He delights in telling you things directly! Yes, there is a different sort of power when you get things from Him directly. The results are more significant and life changing.

Before the seventh seal was opened, God sent one of the great phenomena into earthly places…

Revelation 8:5…*And the angel took the censer, and filled it with the fire of the altar, and cast it into the earth: and there were voices, and thunderings, and lightnings and an earthquake* (KJV)

Among these were *voices*. In the book of Revelation, you would come across two personalities and the usage of the word *voices*. In the first usage, you will come across it in the singular form:

Revelation 4:1...*After this I looked, and, behold, a door was opened in heaven: and the first voice which I heard was as it were of a trumpet talking with me; which said, Come up hither, and I will shew thee things which must be hereafter.* (KJV)

Usually, it would say the *voice* of the Lord or the *voice* of an angel, crying in a loud voice. On other hand, there is the plural usage of the word *'voices'* usually denoting the power of unity. In both usages of this word, we find out that they have come forth to announce the Kingdom of God or to show how God really thinks and the way we humans can line up our thinking pattern with the way God does things.

Revelation 4:5... *And out of the throne proceeded lightnings and thunderings and voices: and there were seven lamps of fire burning before the throne, which are the seven Spirits of God.* (KJV)

'Voices' is the flow of God that sends encrypted messages for the hearer only. Voices are the carriers of words. One thing that is outstanding to know is that visions are made up of words. In other words, to the hearer, He shows words.

In the book of Isaiah, the prophet wrote *...the word that Isaiah the son of Amoz saw concerning Judah*[69]. Amos also said *...the word of Amos, who was among the herdsmen's of Tekoa which He saw concerning Judah*[70].

The Scripture says, *'faith comes by hearing.'* Now, I see the reason why voices were written first in the list. Could it be because all things started from THE VOICE?

THE FORCE OF FAITH

Faith is wrapped up in the words spoken by God to us by and through these voices that are sent to the earthly places. They are not to contradict the written Word of God. You have to be familiar with the written word of the Bible because they would expound the word for you in this last time like they have never done before, with dynamic truths and power. Keep in mind that the Holy Spirit is our Guide and Teacher into all truth.

Without faith, we are nothing! We are saved only by faith.[71] Our justification is by faith[72]. To please God, we need only faith[73]. It is only by faith that we keep

---

[69] Isaiah 2:1

[70] Amos 1:1

[71] Ephesians 2 : 8

[72] Romans 5 : 1

[73] Hebrews 11:6

Christ in our heart.[74] These are not one-time packages, but they are for the daily use in our lives, to bring into existence all that we will ever need.

Faith here is what these sounds of voices are carrying to the body of Christ. If you want these sounds to bring to your faith in the Lord Jesus Christ, then rightly discern the voice. They are all there, speaking at the backdrop, when all the calamities and woes strike on earthly places. God sent voices to bring us truth from the Scripture, to expound some deep things, truth that sets us free and takes away all our burdens.

The Church has never been so sick in the way it is today, sick physically and spiritually. We need the word of the LORD today to liberate us from calamities and deafness.

AUDIONARY LEADERS

Jesus exclaimed at one point when He asked, "when I come will I find faith." The world is asking for faith as well. This is time for the audionary that will desire the raw voice of the Lord. It is here now where power words are conveying in the spirit by voices from heaven.

You may have this burning desire to even hear the audible voice of God at the hour, and I tell you it is possible. Personally, I have heard once the audible voice

---

[74] Ephesians 3 : 17

of God, and it changed my life for good. It was the day of 911 when I was woken up about 3am in the night session, and I heard these words "Alexander, wake up, Pray! The world will never be the same again." Yes, and from that day, it has been a continuous desire to hear accurately in all areas.

In the tenth chapter of the book of Revelation, we see an event before the seventh angel was to blow his trumpet. John saw another angel who came clothed with the cloud and rainbow, his face was as it were the sun and his feet as pillars of fire. He brought down a little book.[75]

This little book may signify brief information of the event to be revealed. Also, it tells us of the unveiling of very quick, brisk, and brief events in history. Yet, it speaks of an extremely monumental and significant event.

This is leading to the seventh angel blowing the seventh trumpet. The descent of this angel came with a cry and a loud voice like that of a lion. And when he cried, the Bible says, he was introduced to the scene of seven thunders.

Now, this is so significant that we are not to gloss over this brief but significant moment. Do you remember what thunder signifies or what they can cause to happen? They bring nations to the worshipful fear of

[75] Revelation 10 : 1-4

the Almighty God. But here it seems as the volume was increased to sound louder than the one that was in the beginning when these great phenomena were introduced.

There were voices of seven thunders that utter these voices of worship in the perfection of holiness. The number seven signifies perfection. So significant is the last of the trumpet to be blown that we behold God ushering in perfection the sounds of worship both of the heavens and of the earth. Hallelujah!

This demonstration shows us how the fear in worshipping the Lord would have to be brought to a higher dimension in our different lives. This time John was eager to write the voices of what he heard, but he was not allowed to do so. Why? Worship is not written, it is captured! It is captured in the heart, in lives, in attitude, in deeds... Oh Lord, may we capture your heart at this time!

The pressure that the world is facing today is of monumental consequences. The earthly realms are about to be shaken by the seven thunderings of God which will be captured within the bowels of man.

John was called up and asked to seal these voices without writing the words but to eat them. *"Then the angel said unto me, 'Take it and eat it up; and it shall make thy belly bitter, but it shall be in thy mouth sweet as honey. And I took the little book out of the angel's hand, and ate it up; and it was in my mouth sweet as honey: and as soon as I had eaten it, my belly was bitter.'"[76]*

The word which the Apostle John ate was sweet to his lips but bitter to his stomach. These end times messages would be sweet to receive from the Lord by so many hearers, but they will be persecuted because the message will be strong and convicting and life-changing. It was bitter in John's belly because he had realized he must say these things that may sound bitter to the body of Christ but are significant and life-changing.

This message that the Apostle John ate must be prophesied. The Apostle Paul says in 1 Corinthians 14: 5, *"I would that ye all spake with tongues, but rather that ye prophesied: for greater is he that prophesieth than he that speaketh with tongues, except he interpret, that the church may receive edifying."*

What we need is this word, which is the voice of loud, quick, strong, and undiluted word of God, to edify the body, to withstand the pressure, the pressure to succumb to the false sound of the world and the onslaught and the devices of the enemy.

This angel told John, *"Thou must prophesy again before many people, and nations and tongues, and kings"* These voices are the sources of powerful strength to be

---

[76] Revelation 10 : 10

given the hearers of our time. They are words that are able to break the sound barrier formed by the enemy of the souls of men. His plans concerning the youth and the young adults of our time can be revealed through these heavenly voices. Voices which are sent by the devil to bring down your body into diseases and conform to the pressure of times, poverty, wars, hate and worldliness, can all be crushed by the voice from above. The angel said to John, *"THOU MUST PROPHESY"*

What must John prophesy? What is the message told unto John? The message to John was, *"Do not write down* but *capture it in the midst of heaven and seal it up* and *put it within you."* Within you dwells God and the power of the Holy Spirit. Within you abides the Spirit of prophecy. So John was asked to eat the sealed voices and the sealed book. In the last days, to John and to all the saints that have an open ear, the sound of the heaven will be revealed and sent forth as prophecy. Prophecy is the word of God spoken from the deepest part of man by faith, through the Holy Spirit.

The message can be best understood when we look at what our Lord and Saviour Jesus Christ pointed out in His last days and realise the end of all things.

And this gospel of the kingdom shall be preached in the entire world for a witness unto all nations; and then shall the end come.[77]

---

[77] Matthew 24:14

97

Voices are the vehicles that transport the last day's message of the kingdom of God to the church. The kingdom message is a mystery, the last mystery that God has in store. It is so wild and big that God brought in the perfection of worship to usher this great message into the world. He said that seven thunders have been lined up to announce this mystery.

Voices declare the Kingdom of God! The book of Revelation says, *"And then the seventh angel sounded: There were great voices in heaven, saying, 'THE KINGDOMS OF THIS WORLD ARE BECOME THE KINGDOMS OF OUR LORD, AND OF HIS CHRIST; AND HE SHALL REIGN FOR EVER AND EVER'"*[78]

These great voices are speaking to the earthly beings in a loud and thunderous noise announcing the kingdom of Our Lord. It is not surprising that this is the only time in Revelation where voices in the plural sense stand alone, and the only word that they announced was **the Kingdom of our Lord.**

All the preparation is worth it. These voices cannot be hindered; they are too loud for the devil to silence them. The Lord sets and prepares the victory before He lets these voices out. They are led by seven thunders and the seventh trumpet sound. This the perfection of worship and time, locked in agreement to usher in the Kingdom of our God. Part of this was captured

---

[78] Revelation 11:15

by John the Baptist, because the Bible prophesied by Isaiah saying, *"the voice of one crying in the wilderness, saying prepare ye the way of the Lord, make his paths straight"*[79]. Jesus soon after He returned from the wilderness where He was fasting and praying for forty days and forty nights with the power of the Holy Spirit, straight away concluded by saying that the kingdom of God is here or is at hand.

The enemy has tried his best and still increasing the volume of our problems, sicknesses, catastrophes, wars, and lies against the Gospel, but they are shut down by the power of the voices of God. You are the generation of hearers whose ears are sanctified for the voices, thunders, lightning, and earthquake of God.

This is a fearful generation! The blurring of the vision of the people of God concerning His word has increased. In medical science, it is called an *Optical Illusion*. God knew that we are going to have this vision. So He had already opened ways which are beyond our imaginations to help us receive His Word without any hindrance. He has sent His word to you; and, His word will clear your vision, add faith to you and establish you.

Yes! He is speaking to you right now! His voice is in your heart; you better have faith in His word. I speak the Word of God to you right now. Receive it in Jesus' precious name! Alleluia!

---

[79] Luke 3: 4

It is His word that will open your ears. Yes! Faith cometh by hearing, hearing by the word of God!

Hearers would crave for His written Word like they never did before in their lives. I challenge you to go back to the Word of God with an open ear, and you will capture the sounds of God!

Job 37: 1-5... *At this also my heart trembleth, and is moved out of his place. Hear attentively the noise of his voice, and the sound that goeth out of his mouth He directeth it under the whole heavens, and his lightning unto the ends of the earth. After it a voice roareth: he thundereth with the voice of his excellency; and he will not stay them when his voice is heard. God thundereth marvelously with his voice; great things doeth he, which we cannot comprehend.*(KJV)

Chapter Fourteen

SOUND WORDS

2 Timothy 1:13...*Hold fast to the form of sound words, which thou hath heard of me, in faith and the love which is in Jesus Christ.* (KJV)

There is a new generation of leaders that God is raising up, a new breed of doers. They are familiar with the voice of the Spirit and led by His sounds. They are hungry for the Word, like never before, and their hearings are sharper than they have ever been. They are not like the fallen Adam who heard the voice of the Lord but tried to hide himself, No! They are like the young Samuel of the days of the fading-eyed Eli, the priest, who when he heard his name being called, came running to him, saying, "Did you call me?"

They would be led not only by means of *spiritual "insights,"* but they will also excel by means of *spiritual "in-sounds."* Their leadership will be termed haphazard and radical, but it has got the signature from heaven. They would be thrust into the front of the battle-lines to lead the people of God.

Their calling will be like that of Samuel. They are called when the Word of the Lord is near, and the eyes of Eli are growing dim. They are called three times in the days of darkness before they wake up. Though timid, God will give them the *Word*. The sound-word cannot drop to the ground; it leads organisations to succeed, and it builds the body of Christ like we all hunger for. Sound-words are righteous words; they deliver us from confusion and separation. They are designed to bring coordination and coherency to the body.

1Sam. 3:6... *And the LORD called yet again, "Samuel." And Samuel arose and went to Eli, and said, "Here am I; for thou didst call me." And he answered, "I called not, my son; lie down again.* (KJV)

This new breed of hearers will be at the cutting edge and innovative. They will have restructured their organisation in the spirit realm before they set out to effect such changes in the physical. They are like Elijah, and they will make sound as *'that by my word.'* Sound words are incredulously personal, and they work aggressively. They are the breeds that will confront the modern reign of Jezebels in the pews, market places, and the government; they are sent by God to destroy the demonic agents from their illegal jurisdictions in earthly places.

They are the weather-changers and the atmospheric thermostat of our time. They switch on the system by force to please their God. By hearing the *'sound of rain,'* Elijah switched on the people of Israel from the demonic system in the kingdom of God to make them ready for an outpouring of the Spirit. If you can hear the sound of outpouring, it will not be a flood. It would only bring a beautiful sight of health, wealth, and restoration of life.

1 Kings 18:41... ***And Elijah said unto Ahab, Get thee up, eat and drink; for there is a sound of abundance of rain.***

It was the perfection of sounds the felled the wall of Jericho. What was Joshua's role? It was to lead the children of Israel into the land of promise, into the land of rest, complete rest, so to speak in the natural. This was the leader who by the instruction, and 'in-sound' into the supernatural works of sounds, believed God. He looked perfectly ridiculous for seven days but kept his ears open to the sound, and he came out with a monumental victory. Yes! *He who has ears, let him hear what the Spirit of the Lord is saying*!

Epilogue

There is a different and more pro-active consciousness in recent times concerning the environment. In many circles, this book carries circumstantial climate conditions shared in heaven and the earth, but it contrasts in the effects incurred.

Sounds Of The Last Days clearly depicts how in heaven, there are earthquakes and thunders, lightning, and great mighty sounds. These also occur in earthly places but with more devastating effects. The natural devastations we are experiencing in recent times are signs and obvious messages on how humanity will live in discomfort until it "wakes up." Romans8:19

BOOKS BY
ALEXANDER O. EMOGHENE

ALEXANDER   EMOGHENE

LOVE IN
ACTION

Encountering Gods manifold dimensions of healing
and power through intimacy

ALEXANDER O
EMOGHENE

GET IN LINE WITH YOUR

DESTINY

A CALL TO THE JOSHUA GENERATION

FIRE RAIN

BREAKING EVIL
CONTAINMENT WITH
PRECISION PRAYERS

ALEXANDER O. EMOGHENE

PERFECTING
LOVE

DEFEATING FEAR THROUGH A SIMPLE UNDERSTANDING
OF THE POWER OF GOD'S LOVE

ALEXANDER O. EMOGHENE

Alexander O. Emoghene

HONGER
NAAR
IMPACT

...IETS STAAT OP HET
PUNT TE VERANDEREN